IMAGINAIRE X

Contemporary Realism

www.fantasmus.com

FANTASMUS PRESENTS

The first book in the "Art of"-series

Contact us on info@fantasmus.com for questions if you want us making a book in this series

Atlantic Empire/Roubloff EU

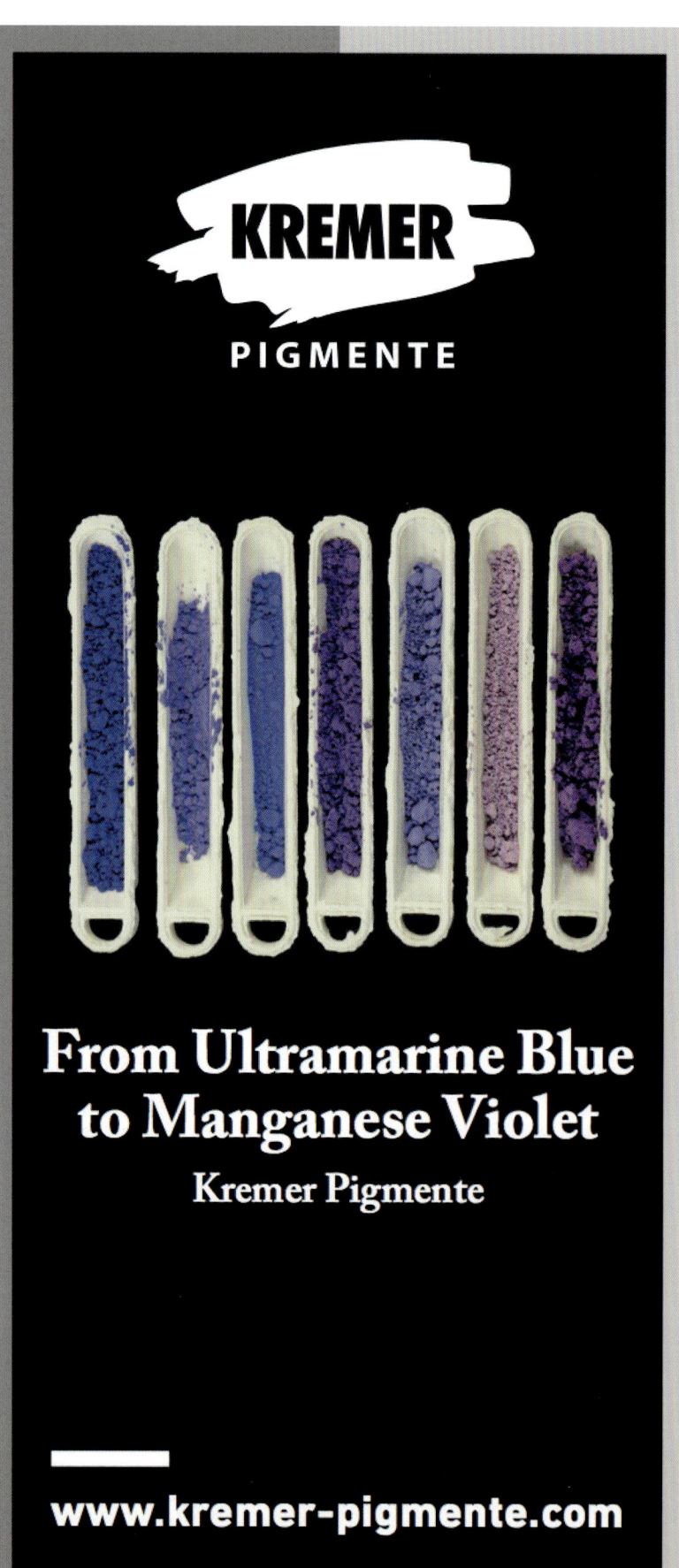

Index

Introduction -
by Mette Torp Bisgaard and Claus Brusen — 4

Nicoletta Ceccoli - *Guest of Honour* — 8

David M. Bowers — 30
Claus Brusen — 34
Ronald Companoca — 40
Helle Rask Crawford — 42
Dominique Desorges — 44
Val Dyshlov — 46
Gabriele Esau — 48
Jacob Gadd — 50
Bjørn Haugaard — 52
Danny Heinricht — 54
Michael Hiep — 56
Joseph Kaliher — 60
Steven Kenny — 62
Patrick van der Linde — 66
Ludmila — 68
Peter van Oostzanen — 70
Flor Padilla — 72
Severine Pineaux — 74
Tim Roosen — 76
Alayne Sahar — 78
Mario Schleinzer — 80
Peter Swift — 82
Cas Waterman — 84
Siegfried Zademack — 86
Olivier Zappelli — 88
Tribute to Patrick J. Woodroffe — 90

Introduction

Time changes, horizons broadens and FANTASMUS acknowledges the way contemporary art develops. And those facts makes it necessary to revise what w have to show and represent while showing art of the present and the future.

Magic realism is so much more than just weird and wacky ways to display well know things and situations in impossible and creative ways. And not just for the artists that produce and unfold the classical styles. Low brow, pop art, pop surrealism, illustration style and many also has their bases in realism with a twist. To embrace that we have chosen to invite all genres that emerge from realism but always with special touch and twist it needs to magic in one way or another.

This edition welcomes Nicoletta Ceccoli as a guest of honour. She's a gifted and highly respected artist pouring her heart and soul out through characters and situations we can all relate to but with the special twist that makes it impossible not to stop and reflect. Always a story and a message hidden in those both cute and horrifying masterpieces. We are proud to be able to show Nicoletta's art in this edition of Imaginaire. And happy to welcome her and many more gifted talents to participate in what we aim to unfold to people throughout the world. These changes makes it possible to widen our horizons and embrace so many wonderful pieces of tales from life.

"Teardrop Pearls"

One of magic realisms great and dedicated protectors sadly passed away on February 13th 2018. A loyal and rock steady support of both art and FANTASMUS. HRH prince Henrik of Denmark. Our Queens husband. It was and will forever be a great loss for both us personally but not the very least the royal family and all of the citizens of Denmark. Prince Henrik was a talented artist himself. He was both a poet and a phenomenal sculptor. Together with our queen he had an exhibition on one of our internationally known museums just a few years ago. Visited by hundreds of thousands in just a few weeks. Prince Henrik was known as an educated, humorous, heartwarming person. And a prankster that always made people laugh. For us the loss is tremendous as we - over the years - got to know him personally and both had him visit us in our home and we visited him in his private chambers in the royal castles. He has been visiting all our exhibitions and he was always the first to get Imaginaire when coming from the printer. He owned many paintings painted by Claus and some of the other artists r presented by FANTASMUS. He has been one of our most loyal guests and clients. Along with being a dedicated and knowing collector of art. Indeed a very special and honourable person. Both as her majesty's husband and as the more private man we met on several occasions.
We've lost an important character.
We will keep our memories dear and enjoy reminiscing about all the joyful moments spend in his company.
May HRH Prince Henrik of Denmark rest in peace.

HRH Prince Henrik visiting FANTASMUS

To celebrate again those important people we've chosen to ad a chapter to the book in which we present to you one of the grand old men of art: Patrick James Woodroffe. Yet another imoprtant spokesman for FANTASMUS. And his family fortunately remains supportive of us.

"Our Den with a Mark"

This 10th edition of Imaginaire is a tribute to art and skills in a broadened perspective.

Thanks to all who've been helping out and making this possible. Especially all of the artists without whom this could never happen, all the readers and fans and all our clients and last but not least our friends, family and supporters.

Enjoy this edition and keep supporting art

Mette Torp Bisgaard, February 2018

FANTASMUS

Yet another year has past and more artists materials have been through our hands to try out and test.

There is not so much doubt that Da Vinci Brushes are among the best. They are fantastic and they are known worldwide, but a few companies, not well known, also deserves some spotlight, especially the Russian brand Roubloff which is gaining more and more its place on the world scene. We now have a European distributor from The Netherlands, so I would expect to see their brushes more and more. Fantasmus is now offering it for sale in our our online store. Another brand which is a small company but with a huge amount of brushes is the Italian Tintoretto. They also produce phenomenal brushes at fair prices, also on stock in our online store. Both Tintoretto and Roubloff have among their line a Master Kolinsky, which is a most fantastic brush for both oil and watercolour. Both are made from the male winter fur which gives the very best brushes, but also the more expensive one. They are really worth it.

On the paint front, we have been sent some different brands to try out. Japanese Kusakabe who makes wonderful paint. They have a series of exclusive oil paints called the guild series. This series is made with the highest concentration of pigments ever. They only have some 12 colours in this series. We received their vermilion which is said to be the best vermilion on the market and its really nice and smooth. Very easy to work with. One of the special thing about their paint is that the pigments particles have been made same size and shape which gives this unique paint- The downside is that its more or less impossible to buy in Europe or the States It is an expensive paint and no one has yet wanted to introduce it here, which is a shame. But perhaps one day!

A good Handmade oil paint which came on the market not so many years ago is Wallace Seymour from England. It is really a very nice paint and prices are reasonable and I have never before seen a bigger variety of earth colours. Huge and many wonderful colours plus many of the ancient colours. But beside the oil paint, WS also makes more or less whatever can be thought of as artistic material. A huge Watercolour program in both pan and tube, historic paints and hyper modern. They have colours for violinmakers, gouache, dry pastel, ancient drawing material, acrylics, inks and mediums of course. Always with the history kept close at heart when making the paints. So far we have the oil colour programme from Wallace Seymour on stock, but hope throughout time to have a wider program as it is a wonderful new addition to the older brands on the market. Pip Seymour keep the pigments special character instead of crushing them so all paint are alike, this can be a challenge if you paint hyperrealism like some of us do, but not impossible. Try them as prices are very reasonable. www.wallaceseymour.co.uk

I also came across a small Austrian producer who still keeps it as a hobby to make oil paint,. The brand is called Lilly Farben. It can only be bought online at www.lilly-farben.at They are good paints and he has a great programme, no exotic colours but the basics which 90% artists need. I was sent samples to try and I liked the quality. I experienced just one problem; it dried too fast for me because he uses siccative. But for some this is fantastic.

I have to mention German Kremer, this company has everything an artist needs if they like to make many materials themselves. They have the largest number of pigments in the western world, they have all you need for working with restoring old paintings, they have the chemicals, the powders...Whatever you need. www.kremer-pigmente.com

On the pastel front, not so much are to be said yet, this is not a field I am at home in. We got a box of "Diana Townsend's Artists' Pastels" and they have nothing to do with cheaper dry pastels you give children or other brands, I have tried before. Diana Townsend makes almost pure pigment sticks. It is a passion for Diana Townsend and has been since she started making those in her kitchen back in 1971. She has constantly worked on her pastels ever since, always trying to improve, despite the high quality. She has kept her knowledge to making pastel and nothing else, which makes her focused on that material. Diana Townsend is from USA, so its an American handmade product of highest quality. www.townsendpastels.com

On the smaller scale of production is Attila Gazo, who is located in USA. He has a small pigment online store www.masterpigments.com in which he sells a variety of the old pigments like Lapis Lazuli which he makes himself from buying the stones and crushes into pigments, but also cleaning according to Cennino Cennini´s recipes from the 14th century. Also a complex procedure for Azurite. He also has some pigments which are only allowed in Europe by professionals at museums, like Orpiment, Leadwhite and Realgar. A very passionate man who knows everything there is to know about pigments. It is not cheap pigments, but you can make sure they are pure, the purest possible. Look on webpage www.masterpigments.com

We shall keep a lookout for small producers who try to make perfection on what they have a passion for.

On the book front there was sent a book from Marcin Kolpanowicz, a retrospective of this amazing Polish artist.
Eli Tiunine, French female artist sent us a book/catalogue called Femme. A nice catalogue displaying her fantastic skills with beautiful but scary paintings.

Claus Brusen
February 2018

NICOLETTA CECCOLI
San Marino
www.nicolettaceccoli.com

Nicoletta Ceccoli was born in Italy in 1973 and graduated from the Institute of Art (Urbino) in 1995, which is located within the resplendent Ducal Palace. The city of Urbino continues to inspire the Artist, influencing her work with its classical beauty. Nicoletta's mountaintop home of San Marino, with its medieval towers and exaggerated perspectives create inspiration for the landscapes of her fairy tale imagination.

Nicoletta is a master of compositional harmony. Through her artistic explorations of love and loss, the Artist illuminates the dark and damaged, rendering them sublime. Soft, endearing colors speak to the subconscious, granting clarity and validation to conflicting emotions.

Nicoletta's work manifests a universe wherein everything that is beautiful is wounded. With soft starkness, she highlights the brutality and muddled nature of the transition of girlhood to womanhood. The Artist's 'Lovely Lolitas' are femme fatales who seduce through veils of chastity.

The pure and innocent color pallet subtly masks desire, repulsion and perversion. Layers of dark symbolism and complexity are presented like a magnificent butterfly collection; exquisite subjects on display to the world, complacently pinned in place by life's cold truths. Hopes of being saved are overwhelmed by the ease of being controlled.

Beneath the alluring imagery, disturbing feelings are intricately examined with a tenderness and beauty that both entices and saddens the viewer. Nicoletta paints a thorough and provocative Beautiful Nightmare in which responsibility withers and expectations remain unfulfilled. The broken pieces of Humpty Dumpty will never be put back together again.

Nicoletta's most recent work explores the myriad, elaborate challenges of relationships; the walls of fear and emotional barricades which are built upon foundations of desire. Nicoletta Ceccoli's career as a children's book illustrator has won worldwide acclaim, and her time in the studio alternates between working for fine art exhibitions and book commissions which have been inspiring children and their parents for decades.

In 2001 Nicoletta was the recipient of the Andersen Prize for Best Italian Illustrator of the Year, and in 2006 she was the recipient of the prestigious silver medal from the Society of Illustrators in New York. She is a four time recipient of the 'Award of Excellence' from Communication Arts, and her art has been exhibited at the Bologna Children's Book fair seven times.

-Heidi Leigh
Owner, AFA Gallery

Lady Bluebell - 50 * 35 cm - acrylics on paper

Leonor - 30 * 30 cm - acrylics on paper

Riddle Princess - 50 * 35 cm - acrylics on paper

Right page:
My Puppy is Scared - 42 * 42 cm - acrylics on paper

A girl hides Secrets - 40 * 29 cm - acrylics on paper

Agata - 50 * 40 cm - acrylics on paper

Love will tear us apart - 35 * 50 cm - acrylics on paper

Octopussy Girl - 30 * 40 cm - acrylics on paper

Ollie Ollie oxen free - 30 * 40 cm - acrylics on paper

Inner self - 30 * 40 - acrylics on paper

The Elephant's Journey - 32 * 42 cm - acrylics on paper

Nascondino - 32 * 42 cm - acrylics on paper

IMAGINAIRE X

Too Fragile - 50 * 40 cm - acrylics on paper

The Princess and the Prey - 50 * 40 cm - acrylics on paper

Just Dessert - 42 * 32 cm - acrylics on paper

Dangerous Liasons - 33 * 45 cm - acrylics on paper

Almost Alice - 21 * 27 cm - acrylics on paper

Persistence in Pink - 58 * 44 cm - acrylics on paper

Soulmate 40 * 30 cm - acrylics on paper

The Ice Princess 44 * 32 cm - acrylics on paper

The Snow Bride - 47 * 42 cm - acrylics on paper

Toyland - 32 * 45 cm - acrylics on paper

IMAGINAIRE X 19

Candy Forest - 30 * 40 cm - acrylics on paper

Consumed by You - 36 * 43 cm - acrylics on paper

Sweet Addiction - 31 * 27 cm - acrylics on paper

20 IMAGINAIRE X

Right page:
All we need is Love - 31 * 31 cm - acrylics on paper

Cuddle - 25 ' 20 cm - acrylics on paper

Bliss - 40 * 30 cm - acrylics on paper

Rose Red 45 * 35 cm - acrylics on paper

Aurora - 35 * 50 cm - acrylics on paper

Arpya - 30 * 40 cm - acrylics on paper

Sheryl - 50 * 40 cm - acrylics on paper and photoshop

Dulcis Agata - 38 * 28 cm - acrylics on paper

Inflorescence - 50 * 40 cm - acrylics on paper

Kathrine - 40 * 35 cm - acrylics on paper

Fight - 30 * 40 cm - acrylics on paper

Right Page:
Dora's Box - 45 * 45 cm - acrylics on paper

Girls don't cry - 30 * 40 cm - acrylics on paper

Lorelei - 40 * 31 cm - acrylics on paper

The Kiss - 30 * 35 cm - acrylics on paper

The peeping Show - 50 * 35 cm - acrylics on paper

Evidently goldfish - 34 * 43 cm - acrylics on paper

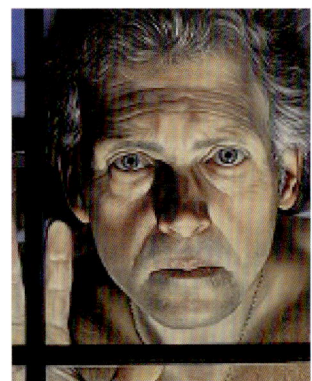

DAVID M. BOWERS
USA
www.dmbowers.com

Second Amendment - 40,5 * 51 cm - oil on Belgian linen

Fountain of Youth - 61 * 61 cm - oil on panel

Sea What I Found - 57 * 44,5 cm - oil on panel

Kingfish - 51 * 40,5 cm - oil on panel

CLAUS BRUSEN
Denmark
www.clausbrusen.com

The Painter - 27 * 23 cm - Oil on panel

Party Animal 3 - Orangutang - 27 * 22 cm - Oil on panel

Cyclop Goat and Meddow Pigs - 27,5 * 23 cm - Oil on panel

Animalesque Botanical Utopism - 32 * 36 cm - Oil on panel

Let me paint the colour of your day - 40 * 30 cm - Oil on panel

Smalt Blue - Air, Moist and Flower - 27 * 22 cm - Oil on panel

Prussian Blue - Air, Moist and Flower - 27 * 22 cm - Oil on panel

Indigo - Air, Moist and Flower - 27 * 22 cm - Oil on panel

Manganese Blue - Air, Moist and Flower - 27 * 22 cm - Oil on panel

IMAGINAIRE X

RONALD COMPANOCA
Peru
www.facebook.com/companocaartworks
www.companoca.blogspot.com

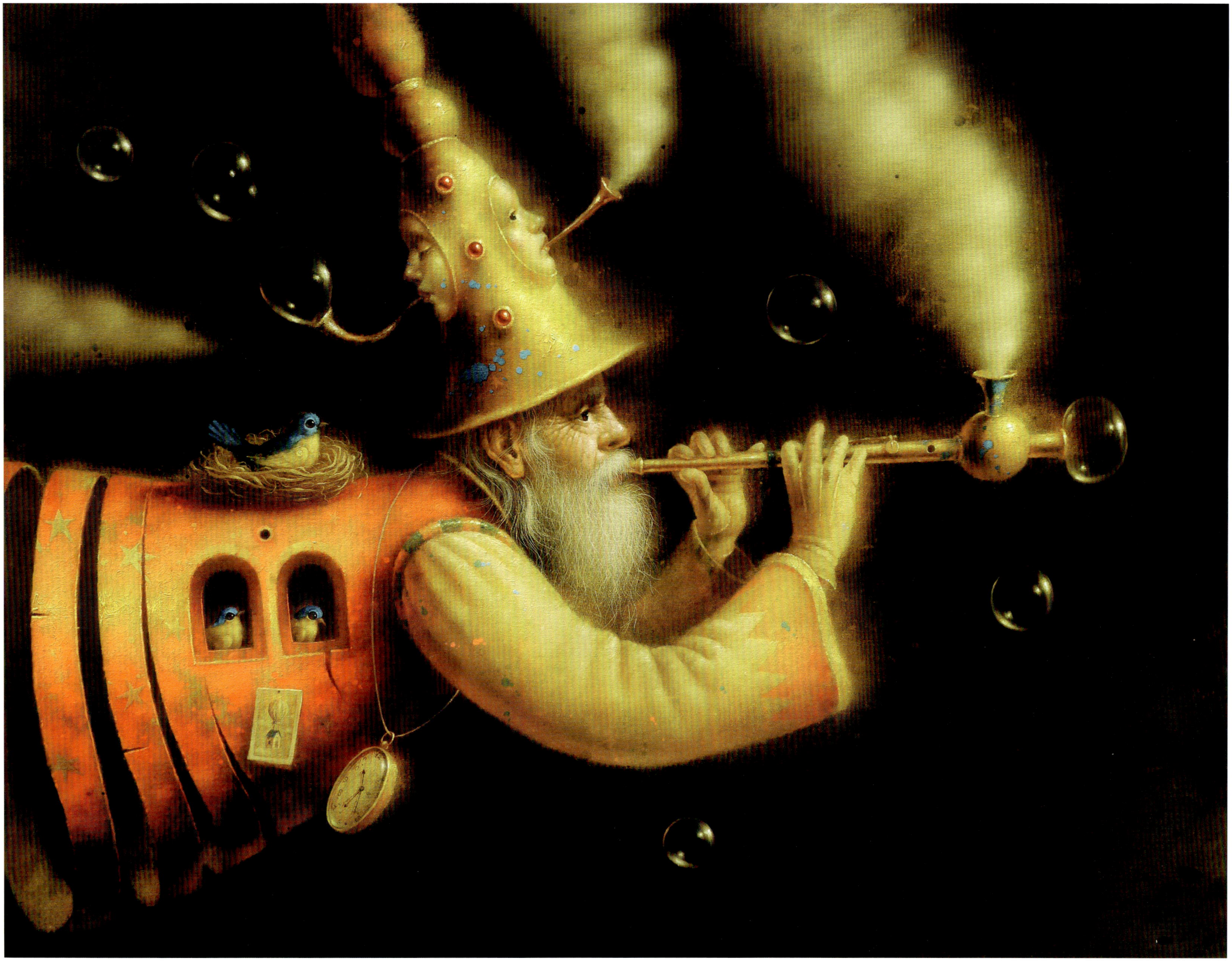

Maker of Clouds - 80 * 100 cm - Oil on canvas

Sueno del relojero - Oil on canvas

HELLE RASK CRAWFORD
Denmark
www.crawfordhouse.dk

Mantiss Fantasies - Bronze

Europa! - Bronze

DOMINIQUE DESORGES
France
www.desorges.fr
www.facebook.com/dominique.desorges

Fusion Cosmique - 133 * 105 cm - Oil on canvas

Larme Solaire - 110 * 110 cm - Oil on canvas

VAL DYSHLOV
USA
dyshlov@gmail.com - www.valdyshlov.com

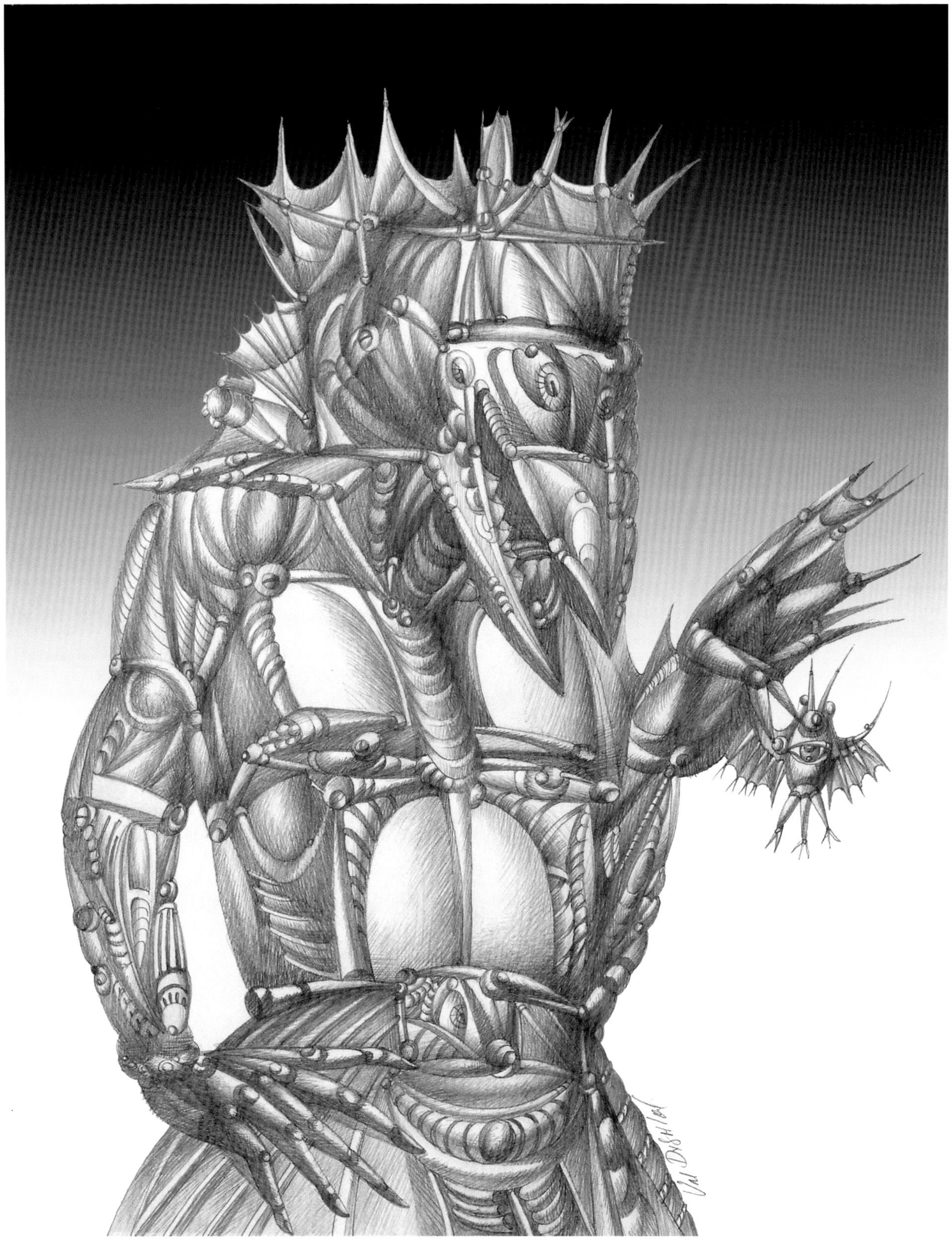

Tressure - 43 * 33 cm - Drawing

Mutation - 43 * 33 cm - Drawing

Argumentation - 43 * 33 cm - Drawing

Congratulation - 33 * 43 cm - Drawing

GABRIELE ESAU
Germany
www.gabriele-esau.de

I missed you - 80 * 60 cm - Oil on canvas

Drosera - 90 * 90 cm - Oil on canvas

JACOB GADD
Denmark
www.jacobgadd.dk

The very kind Walther, the alter ego of Jacob, often manage to get into the picture

The Quartet of Hope - 60 * 80 cm - Acrylics on canvas
(Borad members of Humorism: Ole Fick, Mik Schack, Jacob Gadd, Peter Carlsen)

A Better Day - 50 * 65 cm - Oil on canvas

Hot Stuff - 120 * 200 cm - Acrylics on canvas

Meeting in Jutland - 90 * 120 cm - Acrylics on canvas

BJØRN HAUGAARD
Denmark
www.123hjemmeside.dk/bjoernhaugaard

The Fool -100 * 80 cm - Oil on canvas

Master of Puppets - 100 * 100 cm - Oil on canvas

DANNY HEINRICHT
Denmark
www.dannyheinricht.com

Metaphysical Still Life - 14 * 18 cm - Oil on masonite

Landscape with Rose Hip - 18 * 14 cm - Oil on masonite

MICHAËL HIEP
The Netherlands
www.michaelhiep.com

Little Red Riding Hood - 120 * 90 cm - Oil on linen

Rumpelstiltskin - Detail

Rumpelstiltskin - 120 * 90 cm - oil on linen

JOSEPH WATCHMAN KALIHER
USA/Italy
www. jwk.altervista.org

A story of sufferance and redemption - 60 * 50 cm - Oil on canvas

In the hands of twisted shepherds ! - 60 * 50 cm - Oil on canvas

IMAGINAIRE X 61

STEVEN KENNY
USA
www.stevenkenny.com

The Tornado - 81 * 66 cm - oil on canvas

The Edge - 76 * 56 cm - oil on linen

The Soldier's Daughter - 74.25 * 48.25 cm - oil on panel

The Breaker - 76 * 61 cm - oil on linen

PATRICK VAN DER LINDE
The Netherlands
www.patrickvanderlinde.nl

Venice and the Broken Gondola Chair - 16 * 12 cm - Oil on panel

On Thin Ice - 34 * 24 cm - Oil on panel

Breaking Up - 25,5 * 39 cm - Oil on panel

The Great Drought - 10 * 14 cm - Oil on panel

IMAGINAIRE X 67

LUDMILA
Russia/Portugal
www.ludmila-fantasticart.blogspot.com

She and Her Freedom - 120 * 80 cm - Oil on panel

No title - 30 * 30 cm - Oil on panel

PETER VAN OOSTZANEN
The Netherlands
www.vanoostzanen.com

Done Traveling - 60 * 120 cm - Oil on panel

The God of Flying - 30 * 40 cm - Oil on panel

FLOR PADILLA
Peru
www. florpadilla.blogspot.com

Carrusel Dreams - 34,5 * 23, 5 cm - Oil on linen

Tea Time in the Skye - Hatter - 100 * 70 cm - Oil on linen

Dreams of Freedom - 31 * 25 cm - Oil on linen

SÉVERINE PINEAUX
France
www.pineaux.com

Sacred Deer - The force awakens - 73 * 60 cm - Oil on canvas

Duale - Ø 80 cm - Oil on canvas

TIM ROOSEN
Belgium
www.timroosen.be

"Nezera", mild steel, wrought iron and copper, life size

Pictures by Ansgar Noeth and Iris Bitter

"Felicia", mild steel and brass, life size

ALAYNE SAHAR
USA

www.alaynesahar.art
www.facebook.com/Alayne-Abrahams-1293602242596331/

Even Guardian Angels Get the Blues - 35,5 * 50,8 cm - Watercolour

Night Flight - 50,8 * 35,5 cm - Watercolour

The Ascent - 50,8 * 35,5 cm - Watercolour

Rose Reverie - 50,8 * 35,5 cm - Watercolour

IMAGINAIRE X 79

MARIO SCHLEINZER
Austria
www.mario-s.bplaced.net

Life Isn´t A Game - 40 * 50 cm - Coloured pencil, acrylic and oil on hardboard

Atom Heart Mother - 29 * 29 cm - Acrylic and Oil on Hardboard

Bright Look Out - 50 * 40 cm - Colored pencil, acrylic and oil on hardboard

The Blossom Of Love In Protection - 30 * 23 cm - Acrylic and Oil on hardboard

Departure - 30 * 40 cm - Coloured pencil, acrylic and oil on hardboard

IMAGINAIRE X 81

PETER SWIFT
USA
www.peterswiftartstudio.com

Chesapeake Bay Blue Crab - 61 * 91 cm - Oil on canvas

Eight Carrots - 152 * 152 cm - Acrylic on canvas

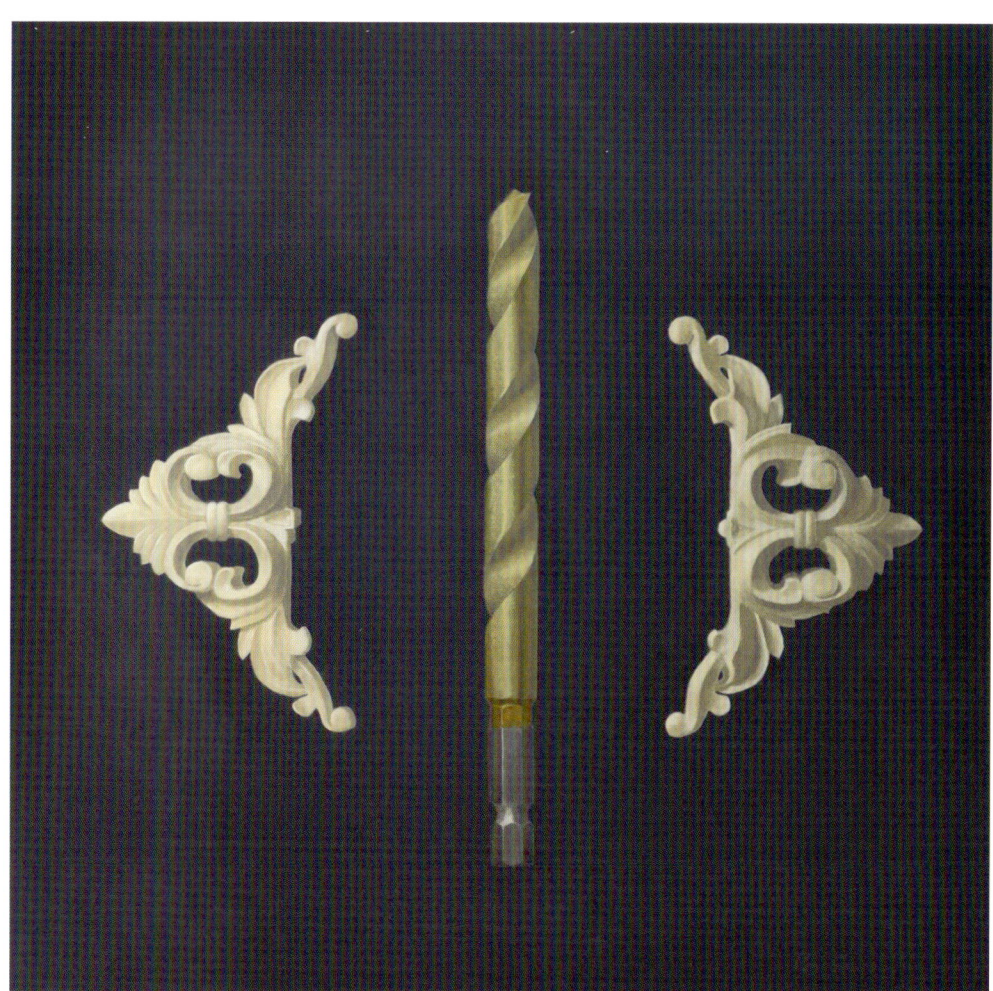
Drill Bit and Ornamental Wood - 122 * 122 cm - Oil on canvas

Eight Baseballs - 152 * 152 cm - Acrylic on canvas

Sleigh Bells and Hornets - 152 * 152 cm - Acrylic on canvas

IMAGINAIRE X 83

CAS WATERMAN
The Netherlands
www.caswaterman.nl

The taste of Sweet - 30 * 20 cm - Oil on panel

The taste of Salt - 30 * 20 cm - Oil on panel

The Border - 70 * 40 cm - Oil on canvas

Zaou - 30 * 20 cm - Oil on panel

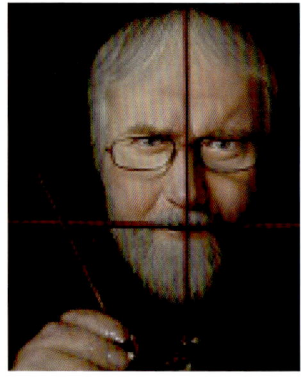

SIEGFRIED ZADEMACK
Germany
www.zademack.com

The black sun - 60 * 72 cm - Oil on canvas

Charon - 90 * 60 cm - Oil on canvas

OLIVIER ZAPPELLI
Switzerland
www.zappelli.ch

Good Soup - Ø 123 cm - Oil on board

Edible Flower - Ø 122 cm - Oil on board

Tribute to Patrick James Woodroffe
27/10-1940 - 10/5-2014

Some 4 years ago one of the most significant artist in magic realism passed away. Patrick James Woodroffe was in many ways a brilliant genious. When entering his world you will be sorrounded by the Land of Make Believe. And nothing else seems to matter. And this very special place was also Patrick's personal sanctuary. A getaway from the unfriendly world we are all being a part of. In many ways he did what all children do and what many more adults should do from time to time. Escape into places where everything is good and nothing bad can harm you.

To me Patrick's many pieces of art mean something special, as they always seem to pull me into a calm and very soulfull state of mind. Every piece is a small fairy tale that still surprises me every time I look at it. The details are endless and his techniques in painting were brilliant. The atmosphere is dragging me into all the different places. Make my mind wander for a while. Calling for peace and leaving me in a very special mood. Whether it's been meeting some of the pleasent characters or having been taken to beautiful places, it's always with a good feeling having visited Patrick's world. In so many ways I can relate to his world. Especially growing up with the fairy tales of H.C.Andersen and having loved Lewis Carroll's authorship. Specifically Alice in Wonderland. Patrick seems to capture all the best of all worlds in his own way and in his very special world.

Patrick himself stated that:
" I feel at home in my own imagery. I live in a world of my own, a planet with portraits and landscapes far too pretty to be called "modern art". My "Text & Images", which come just from my memories and my imagination, are nearly always limited to optimism. Tragic stories and ugly imagery never make me happy...."

This and much more, along with many of his masterpieces you can see visiting his webpage, which his wife Jean Woodroffe keeps alive in loving memory of her late husband.

www.patrickwoodroffe-world.com

In this art Patrick's spirit lives forever and for that many of us are grateful.

Hortus Conclusus - oil on panel

The Coastal Footpath - 61 * 61 cm - oil on panel
Right page in an upside down version. Signed both ways

The Sentinel - oil on panel
Cover for Pallas-album

Trespasser will be Welcome - oil on panel

Beware the Frumious Bandersnatch - oil on panel

Alicia and Sarah - oil on panel

IMAGINAIRE X

Death of the Air - oil on panel

Tinker says Goodbye - oil on panel

Pastures in the Sky - oil on panel

FANTASMUS PRESENTS
THE IMAGINAIRE SERIES

Check at www.fantasmus.com for the whole series and many more

IMAGINAIRE X

Contemporary Realism

First published in Denmark 2018
Copyright © 2018 FBB-FANTASMUS Bisgaard Brusen - FANTASMUS Artbooks

First edition

All rights reserved to the publisher. No part of this book may be reproduced or transmitted in any form, mannor or media including photography, recording or any other information storage and retrieval system, nor may pages be applied to any material, cut, trimmed or sized to alter the excisting trim sizes matted or framed with the intent to create other products for sale or resale or profit in any manor whatsoever, withour prior permission in writing from the publisher and/or the artists.

IMAGINAIRE X
2018 , with reg.
ISBN: 978-87-970439-0-5
EAN: 9788797043905
ISSN: 1903-7708

Introduction by Mette Torp Bisgaard

Special thanks to Nicoletta Ceccoli
Thanks to Claus Brusen
Set in Adobe Garamond Pro
Design and Layout by Mette Torp Bisgaard, FANTASMUS

Cover: Nicoletta Ceccoli - Consumed by You
Backside: A mix of what's inside

www.fantasmus.com

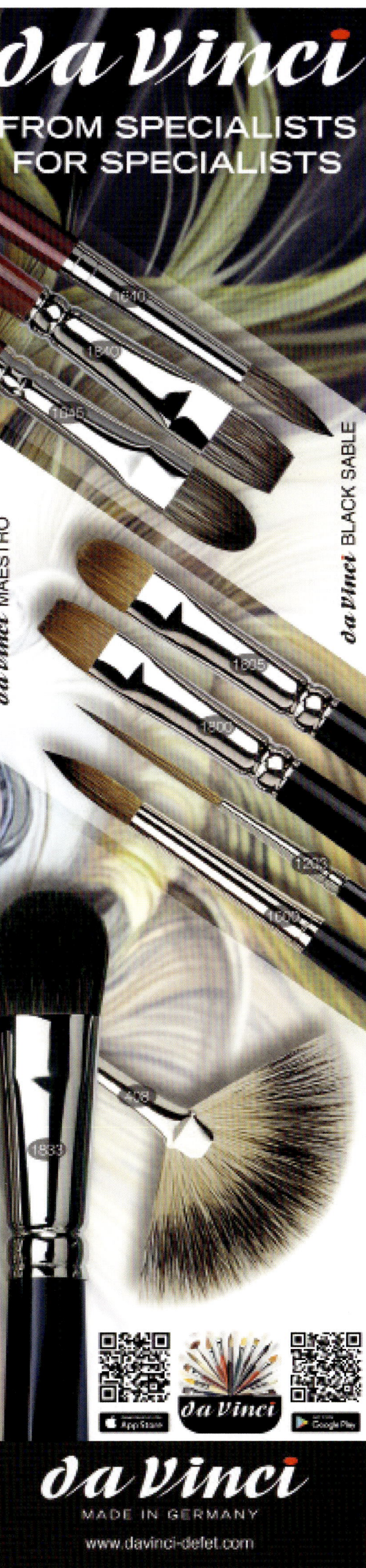